PASTOR FUNKE ADERINOLA

GOD IS ABLE

Table of Contents

Other Titles By

Pastor Funke Aderinola

1. 30 Days Prayers For Next Level
2. 30 Days Prayers That Will Bring Transformation
3. 30 Days Prayers To Make You Become An Achiever
4. Changing The Unchangeable
5. Detach Yourself from Self-Imposed Yokes
6. Fasting and Praying
7. Put Away Strange gods

The titles above can be purchased from:

www. bodyofchristchristiancentre.com

You can follow Pastor Funke via the Body of Christ Centre Facebook page. You will find daily live and recorded messages that will bless and enrich your Christian walk.

www.facebook.com/BodyOfChristChristianCentre

Written by Pastor Funke Aderinola

Edited by Prince Kambale

Produced in the United Kingdom of Great Britain and Northern Ireland.

ISBN 978-1-908228-10-9

Jointly Published by
Chrisfun Publishers & Logos To Rhema Publications

Bible Versions used:

Unless stated otherwise, all scripture quotations in this book are taken from New King James Versions of the Holy Bible.

INTRODUCTION

God, who is the creator of all things, the Lord Almighty is the able God. He is God by Himself. He is not one of the gods but He is Eternal. He is the creator that is not created by anyone or anything. He is the Lord from the beginning to the end. He is called the Alpha and the Omega. There is no place for argument, He is just God all by Himself.

God is bigger than the biggest. He is higher than the highest. He is stronger than the strongest. He is richer than the richest. He is wiser than the wisest. He is greater than the greatest. He is mightier than the mightiest. He is ageless, peerless, matchless, endless and timeless. There are insufficient words to describe Him. He is the indescribable God. He is incomparable and God's ability is inexhaustible.

He is the Lord. There is nothing He cannot do.

Ephesians 3:20 says " *Now to Him who is able to do exceedingly abundantly above all that we ask or think, according to the power that works in us,"*

Beloved of God, I want you to know that there is nothing that is a challenge to you that God cannot fix. God is more than able to turn every barren situation to fruitfulness. He is able to make a way where there is no way. He is the unchangeable changer. *For with Him nothing shall be impossible.* (Luke 1:37). He can be trusted because He can never mismanage our lives.

God is the capable God. He is able to change times and seasons. Fix your mind on Him and you will never be disappointed.

I see you rising to your next level. This is your season of change, in Jesus name. Every mountain shall be scattered. Your season of reproach is over. The able God will step into every situation of your life and you will become a testimonial, in Jesus name.

As you read this book, your faith will rise to the next level. *The bible says faith comes by hearing and hearing by the word of God.* (Romans 10:17).

Read and be blessed, in Jesus name.

CHAPTER 01

WHO IS GOD?

God is indescribable. He is ageless, endless and timeless. Man can only try and describe who God is according to man's revelation of God. No man has the capacity to describe God fully. Man can only try to be able to describe God, it is needful to look through the bible, the living word of God.

God Is The Creator

In Genesis 1:1 the Bible says,
"In the beginning God created the heavens and the earth...."

God is the creator of the universe. All things were made by

Him and without Him was not anything made.

Revelation 4:11 declares:
"You are worthy, our Lord and God,to receive glory and honour and power, for you created all things, and by your will they were created and have their being."

Also, man is created in the image and in the likeness of God.(Genesis 1:27). Everything that is in existence today is created by God.

The Almighty

God is the Almighty God. In other words, He is the all powerful, omnipotent, supreme, unequalled and peerless God. In Genesis 17:1, God introduced Himself to Abraham as the Almighty God. God said,
"I am the Almighty God; walk before me and be thou perfect."

God was telling Abraham that He is the utmost, the one who is supreme. At this time in Abraham's life, Abraham was going through a difficult period. He was ninety nine years old and his wife was eighty nine years old without a child. The Almighty reassured Abraham that He the Lord is able to do all things and for Abraham to experience His mightiness, he must walk before He the Lord and be perfect. God is truly the Almighty God. He proved Himself in Abraham's life. Sarah, Abraham's wife conceived.The bible says in Genesis:21:1-7,

"[1] And the Lord visited Sarah as He had said, and the Lord did for Sarah as He had spoken. [2] For Sarah conceived and bore Abraham a son in his old age, at the set time of which God had spoken to him. [3] And Abraham called the name of his son who was born to him—whom Sarah bore to him—Isaac. [4] Then Abraham circumcised his son Isaac when he was eight days old, as God had commanded him. [5] Now Abraham was one hundred years old when his son Isaac was born to him. [6] And Sarah said, "God has made me laugh, and all who hear will laugh with me." [7] She also said, "Who would have said to Abraham that Sarah would nurse children? For I have borne him a son in his old age."

God's supreme power was manifested in the life of Abraham and his wife. In Genesis 24:1 the bible says Abraham was old and well stricken in years and the Lord had blessed Abraham in all things. He experienced the unlimited power of God. Hallelujah.

God Almighty wants to prove His mightiness in your life today. Walk before God. Live a life of holiness. Mathew 5:48 says, *"Be ye perfect as your Heavenly Father is perfect."* To experience the supreme power of God, you must have the mind of Christ. (Philippians 2:5). Choose to walk with God with a heart of purity. No one can do that for you. It is a choice every individual must make. God wants you and l to live a life of purity. He died for mankind so that we can be free from sins. The word of God declares that God so loved the world that He gave His only begotten son to die for mankind and whosoever believes in Him will not perish but have eternal life. (John3:16). Jesus died for you and I to be free from sin and experience eternal life.

Most High God

God is the most high that is higher than the highest. He is above everything, nothing is higher than Him.

Psalms 91:1 says, *"He who dwells in the secret place of the Most High Shall abide under the shadow of the Almighty."*

God is higher than your problems and your needs. At the mention of His name every knee must bow. There is nothing that is challenging your faith that God is not above. He is the most high God. He is superior to every need of man. It is important for you to abide under the shadow of the Almighty God. Hang on Him in every situation, you will never be disappointed, He is the most high God.

God is all

God is all in all. He is the absolute God. Colossians 3:11 says, *"Christ is all and in all."*

In Him we are complete.Without Him we are nothing.

Colossians 2:10 says, *"and you are complete in Him, who*

is the head of all principality and power."

New Living Translation Bible says, *"So you are also com plete through your union with Christ, who is the head over every ruler and authority."*

Are you complete in Christ? Have you given your totality to Jesus?

It is profitable for man to surrender all to Jesus. Never hold back from the Lord, He is our all in all. Receive grace to surrender all to Him today.

The all knowing God.

One of the attributes of God is that He knows all things. He is the omniscient God. He is well informed about everything because He created all things. He is boundless, infinite, unlimited and all seeing. Nothing is hidden from Him. He knows our going out and our coming in. You and I cannot hide from Him. Hebrews 4:13 says, *"And there is no creature hidden from His sight, but all things are open and made bare to the eyes of Him."*

All things are open to God. The Psalmist says in Psalms 139:7-12: " [7] *Where can I go from Your Spirit? Or where*
can I flee from Your presence? [8]*If I ascend into heaven, You*
are there; If I make my bed in hell, behold, You are there.
[9]*If I take the wings of the morning, And dwell in the ut-*
termost parts of the sea, [10]*Even there Your hand shall lead*
me, And Your right hand shall hold me. [11]*If I say, "Surely*
the darkness shall fall on me," Even the night shall be light
about me; [12]*Indeed, the darkness shall not hide from You,*
But the night shines as the day; The darkness and the light
are both alike to You. [13]*For You formed my inward parts;*
You covered me in my mother's womb."

God knows everything. He is the all knowing God. Jeremiah 23:24 says, *"Can anyone hide himself in secret places, So I shall not see him?" says the Lord; "Do I not fill heaven and earth?" says the Lord."*

How do you live your life? Are you aware that God sees everything and knows everything? Your life is not hidden from Him and you are not a surprise to God. Live daily with the consciousness of God seeing everything.

God is faithful

God is a faithful God. He is reliable, trustworthy, dependable, He is ever true to His words. He is constant, steadfast, unchanging, unwavering.

1 Corinthians 1:9 says, *"God is faithful, by whom you were called into the fellowship of His Son, Jesus Christ our Lord."*

God is ever faithful. He called us as His own, He will establish us and also save us from evil. (2 Thessalonians 3:3). As a child of God, are you faithful to God in all that you do? Are you faithful in your service to God? Are you faithful to your family ? Are you faithful at your place of work? Are you a faithful person? As children of God we must be found faithful in all things. The word of God declares in 1 Corinthians 4:1-2 that *"Our God is faithful so we must be faithful in all things."*

The bible says we have the *mind of Christ.* (1 Corinthians 2:16). We are encouraged by the word of God to be like our God. The bible says, in Philippians 2:5: *"Let this mind be in you, which was in Christ Jesus."*

Beloved of God, be faithful to God in everything that you do. Faithfulness is profitable. The bible says in Proverbs 28:20 : *that a faithful man will abound with blessings.*

Do you want to experience unlimited blessings? God wants you to be blessed. That is why at creation in Genesis 1:26 the bible says, *"And God said, Let us make man in our image, after our likeness: and let them have dominion over the fish of the sea, and over the fowl of the air, and over the cattle, and over all the earth, and over every creeping thing that creepeth upon the earth."*

Dear child of God, be faithful to God in all things so that you can experience God's blessings.

God is powerful

God is the powerful, unlimited God. He is supreme and nothing can restrict Him. He has the power to do all things.

Psalms 62:11 says, *"God has spoken once, Twice I have heard this: That power belongs to God."*

He is the omnipotent God, all power belongs to Him.

Mathew 28:18 says, " *And Jesus came and spoke to them, saying, "All authority has been given to Me in heaven and on earth.* [19] *Go therefore and make disciples of all the nations, baptising them in the name of the Father and of the Son and of the Holy Spirit,* [20] *teaching them to observe all things that I have commanded you; and lo, I am with you always, even to the end of the age. Amen."*

We are created in the image and likeness of God. We are created to be like Him. God is powerful, so are we. Mathew 28:19 says, "go ye therefore..." The bible is telling us that children of God have unlimited power just as our creator is. Do you know how powerful you are? You and l are created to be powerful. Luke 10:19 says,"*Behold, I give you the authority to trample on serpents and scorpions, and over all the power of the enemy, and nothing shall by any means hurt you."*

Children of God are supposed to be carriers of God's power. When Jesus was about to leave His disciples He told them to wait in Jerusalem until they received power from on high. In Acts 2, the disciples prayed in the upper room and they were all baptised with the Holy Ghost and fire. They received power from above and they became world changers. You are a world changer by birth, begin to walk in that realm, in Jesus name. I see you doing exploits for the Lord, Amen.

God is love

God is a loving father. From the beginning God loves man with an everlasting love. (Jeremiah 31:3). His love for man is unconditional. John 3:16 says,
" For God so loved the world that He gave His only begotten Son, that whoever believes in Him should not perish but have everlasting life."

He loves man so much that He sent His only son to die for us. The bible says He first loved us. While we were yet sinners, He died for mankind. Beloved of God, do you realise how much God loves you?

The Psalmist says in Psalms 25:6,
Remember, O Lord, Your tender mercies and Your loving

kindnesses, For they are from of old."

You and I are the beloved of God. He said in Malachi 1:2, *"I have loved you."*

God loves you and I, there is no doubt about this. He loves us first before we love Him.

My question to you today is, do you love God? How hot is your love for Him? Do you have a burning desire for Him?

Deuteronomy 6:5 says, *You shall love the Lord your God with all your heart, with all your soul, and with all your strength."*

If you love God, you will make Him your priority, you will not allow anything or anyone to take His place in your life. Also, love for God will make you obey Him at all times.

John 14:15 says, *"If you love Me, keep My commandments.*

Are you obeying God? Dear child of God, obeying Him is profitable. One of the advantages of obeying God is in John 3:22 that says, *" And whatever we ask we receive from Him, because we keep His commandments and do those things that are pleasing in His sight."*

If you want God to respond to your cry, obedience is the key. If you truly love Him, obey Him. I see God catapulting you into your breakthrough as you obey His words.

Love for God will make you love people, especially children of God. The bible says that we must love as Christ loves. If you really know God, you will not hate anyone.

1 John 4:7-16 says, "[7] *Beloved, let us love one another, for love is of God; and everyone who loves is born of God and knows God.* [8] *He who does not love does not know God, for God is love.* [9] *In this the love of God was manifested toward us, that God has sent His only begotten Son into the world, that we might live through Him.* [10] *In this is love, not that we loved God, but that He loved us and sent His Son to be the propitiation for our sins.* [11] *Beloved, if God so loved us, we also ought to love one another.* [12] *No one has seen God at any time. If we love one another, God abides in us, and His love has been perfected in us.* [13] *By this we know that we abide in Him, and He in us, because He has given us of His Spirit.* [14] *And we have seen and testify that the Father has sent the Son as saviour of the world.* [15] *Whoever confesses that Jesus is the Son of God, God abides in him, and he in God.* [16] *And we have known and believed the love that God has for us. God is love, and he who abides in love abides in God, and God in him."*

Beloved of God, I pray that you will always love God and

the people He created in His image and likeness, in Jesus name. Amen.

God is the Lord of Host

The Lord Almighty is the Lord of host. In Haggai 2:4-9, the Lord was called the Lord of Host 4 times. He is a mighty man of war. (Exodus 15:3). He has never lost a battle and He will never lose a battle. The word of God declares in Isaiah 42:13:

"The Lord shall go forth like a mighty man; He shall stir up His zeal like a man of war. He shall cry out, yes, shout aloud; He shall prevail against His enemies."

Our father is a mighty warrior who can never be defeated. As children of a warrior, we are warriors too. You and I can never be defeated. The bible says we are more than a conqueror through Christ that loved us. (Romans 8:37). The Lord of hosts is on our side. If God is for us, who can be against us? Nothing. Our defence is the Lord of hosts.

God is able to do.

The Lord is able to do, that is He is the doer of all things. He is more than capable and proficient. He has what it takes to sort out all issues of life. He is the ultimate. He alone can do what no man can do and He has the ability to accomplish what no man can accomplish. He has no equals. He alone is more than able. Ephesians 3:20 declares,
" Now to Him who is able to do exceedingly abundantly above all that we ask or think, according to the power that works in us,

It is important that our words and thoughts are in line with the word of God because God will respond exceedingly and abundantly to everyone's words and thoughts. Dear child of God, God will surely respond to you. He is a loving father that wants the best for you. Ask and

you will receive, seek and you will find, knock and the door shall be opened unto you (Mathew7:7). There is nothing too big or too small for God to do, just come boldly before Him and you will see God doing wonders in your life. Never underestimate the power of the able God. Tell Him your heart desires today and He will do more for you in Jesus name. I see God changing your story around for a miracle and you shall become the envy of men in Jesus name. Glory be to God.

CHAPTER 02

GOD IS ABLE TO FORGIVE SINS.

The ability of God is unlimited. He is more than capable. He can do all things and that is why we call Him he able God. In light of the power at work within us, God is ıble to accomplish exceedingly, abundantly over all we ask ›r imagine. (Ephesians 3:20). God sent His son Jesus Christ o die for our sins. The blood shed on the cross of Calvary s for the remission of our sins. Some people believe that hey have gone too far in sin that the blood of Jesus cannot edeem them. Isaiah 1:18 says,

'Come now, and let us reason together," Says the Lord, Though your sins are like scarlet, They shall be as white

as snow; Though they are red like crimson, They shall be as wool."

Confess your sins today and the blood of Jesus will make you clean as white as snow. Jesus paid the price for you and I on the cross of Calvary. He knew no sin, He was made sin because of our sins. God loves us so much, He sent His only begotten Son to die on the cross. You and I must no continue in our sins, Jesus went to the cross to redeem us

The bible says in 2 Corinthians 5:21 says,
" For He made Him who knew no sin to be sin for us, tha we might become the righteousness of God in Him."

Therefore, whosoever shall call upon the name of the Lord shall be saved from the grip of sin. Jesus came to save us

Romans 10:9-10 says,
"9 that if you confess with your mouth the Lord Jesus and believe in your heart that God has raised Him from the dead, you will be saved. 10 For with the heart one believes unto righteousness, and with the mouth confession is made unto salvation."

God loves us so much that He shed His blood for us. He

paid the highest price for our redemption. God is the Alpha and Omega. He is the beginning and the end that knows all things. Over 2000 years ago, Jesus went to the cross to die for mankind. Through the blood of Jesus Christ man's sins were forgiven yesterday and He is still forgiving man"s sins today, and He will still forgive sins tomorrow. He is the same God yesterday, today and forever. He is a forgiving father. Jesus came to save us.

When Jesus was on earth many came to Him and He forgave all that came to Him for a renewal of life, He is still renewing lives today and forever. Praise the Lord. Accept the redemptive work of Jesus today. Come to Jesus the way you are, He loves you and He is interested in your well being. He wants His children to be as He is holy.

Examples of those whose sins were forgiven

WHEN JESUS WAS ON EARTH.

1. ZACCHAEUS, THE TAX COLLECTOR

In Luke Chapter 19:1-10, the bible says that one day Jesus came to Jericho and there was a man called Zacchaeus, who was a chief tax collector. He sought to see Jesus but because he was a short man he could not see Jesus because of the large crowd. The bible says that Zacchaeus ran ahead of the crowd and climbed onto a sycamore tree in order to see Jesus. When Jesus got to the place where Zacchaeus was, Jesus asked him to come down and told Zacchaeus that He would be coming to his house that day. Zacchaeus was more than willing although the people were not happy about it because they knew Zacchaeus was a cheater. That very day salvation came into Zacchaeus' house. He made a turn around from his sinful ways because he had an encounter with Jesus, the Saviour. He changed from being a cheat to an honest man. Thank God that the son of man came to seek and save sinners. Hallelujah.

No one has to die in his or her sins. Acts 2:21 says that anyone that will call upon the name of the Lord shall be saved. It is profitable to live a righteous life. The bible says in Proverbs 11:4b that *"but righteousness delivereth from death."* How are you living your life? Is your life in line with the word of God? Do you have the mind of Christ? The bible says that if any man be in Christ, he is a new creature, old things have passed away, all things will become new. Are you living the new life in Christ?

No man's sin is too grievous that Jesus cannot forgive. If you are not living right, go before Jesus and confess all your sins today. He is faithful and just to forgive all sins. He loves you and He cares about you.

Surrender all to Jesus today. I see God beautifying your life, in Jesus name.

2. Mary Magdalene had seven evil spirits

According to Luke 8:1-2, the bible says that when Jesus was on earth, He preached to many sinners and among them were women who got delivered from evil spirits and one of those women was Mary Magdalene who was delivered from seven evil spirits. Prior to her encounter with Jesus, she was living in sin but the moment she had an encounter with Jesus, she was delivered from her sinful ways and followed Jesus all the way.

In Mark 16:9 it was recorded that after Jesus died on the cross of Calvary and was buried and He resurrected, the first person He appeared to was Mary Magdalene. This shows that there is no one God cannot save, that is why the bible says that even if our sins are as red as scarlet they shall be as white as snow and if they are as red as crimsons, t shall be as wool. (Isaiah 1:18). No man has to die a sinner, 'esus paid the price on the cross for our redemption. Today go to Jesus with a humble heart and let Him cleanse you otally.

3. The Samaritan woman at the well

esus came to Jericho in John Chapter 4 and He sat by the well because He was weary. The bible says a Samaritan woman saw Jesus and Jesus asked her for a drink but the woman was surprised because the Jews had no dealings with the Jews at that time. Jesus told the woman that He is he one that gives the living water and if she would ask for he living water, she would never thirst again and the water will be a well of water springing into everlasting life. She said, *"Sir, give me this water, that I thirst not, neither come hither to draw."* Jesus, all knowing, began to tell the woman the story of her life and the woman perceived that He is the Messiah.The disciples came and saw the woman and they were surprised that Jesus was talking with a Samaritan woman. Jesus came to save the lost. That day, the woman's life was changed and the bible says, she went and called the whole city to come and see Jesus. She had an encounter with Jesus, instantly she became a soul winner. The bible says, i any man be in Christ, he is a new creature, old things have passed away and all things have become new. (2 Cor inthians 5:17). An encounter with Jesus changes everything I pray for you today that you will never miss your day o encounter, in Jesus name. Amen.

4. The impotent man at the pool of Bethsaida

In John chapter 5:1-9 the bible says, there was an impoten man, in the midst of sick folks by the pool of Bethsaida. Al of them by the pool were waiting for the moving of the wa ter to get their healing because the angel of the Lord would move the water and whoever would get in first would be made whole. The impotent man by the pool had been there for 38 years, hoping it would be his day one day.

God is the master planner, He knows what to do concerning every situation. He is the able God that can do all things.

Jesus the healer located the impotent man by the pool. The man did not even know that it was his day of visitation. Jesus asked him, *" do you want to be made whole?"* Instead of saying a big yes, he was telling Jesus of how he had been waiting for the moving of the water and how another man would have stepped in before him.

May you recognise your day of visitation in Jesus name.

Thank God for His mercy. Jesus commanded the man to take up his bed and the man did and instantly the man who was bedridden for thirty eight years received his miracle and was healed of his infirmity. In addition, Jesus told the man to sin no more. The man received mercy. His sins were forgiven by the master.

God sent His son Jesus to the world for the forgiveness of our sins.

5. Saul of Tarsus

As stated in Acts 8, Saul was a persecutor of the Christian. It was recorded in Acts 7:58 that when Stephen was being stoned, the people laid their garments at Saul's feet. One day the great persecutor was met by the Lord on the way to Damascus where he wanted to go and persecute more Christians. He had an encounter with the Lord, his sins were forgiven and his life was changed and he became a great witness for the Lord. Saul, who was also called Paul, described himself as a chief sinner.

The Mercy of God located him and he became a mighty

tool in the hand of God. The chief sinner became one of the Apostles in the New Testament.

The word of God is true. The bible says, in 2 Corinthians 5:17, *"If any man be in Christ, he is a new creature, old things are passed away, all things are become new."*

God did many signs and wonders through Apostle Paul because he had an encounter with Jesus.

A genuine follower of God is unable to continue on with their sinful ways on a regular basis! It's not possible ! It is quite probable that an individual who professes to be a child of God yet persists in their sinful ways was never truly born again.

The Bible makes it quite evident that a sincere follower of God cannot ever live a life filled with sin!

1 John 3:6 says,
"Whosoever abideth in him sinneth not: whosoever sinneth hath not seen him, neither known him."

God wants all His children to live a life of purity.

Yield yourself to Him today, let Him prove Himself in your life. He wants to turn you into a wonder, to your world. Make up your mind to forsake sin totally and by the grace that is in Christ Jesus, begin to live a life of purity.

CHAPTER 03

GOD IS ABLE TO BLESS YOU.

The All-Powerful God is the One Who Can Do Anything. There is nothing too hard for Him to do. God s the God of blessings. He is the God that blesses. When God created man, He pronounced blessings upon man right from the beginning. The bible says in Genesis chapter one that God created man in His image and likeness and after creation God blessed them and said, *"be fruitful, and multiply and replenish the earth, and subdue it: and have dominion…."* (Genesis 1:28). It is God's master plan for His children to be blessed. Jeremiah 29:11 says,

'For I know the thoughts that I think toward you, saith he LORD, thoughts of peace, and not of evil, to give you an expected end."

One of the plans of God for your life is to be blessed. God wants you to be blessed in your going out and in your coming in. You and I are destined to be blessed. That is why the word of God in 3 John 2 says, *"Beloved, I wish above all things that thou mayest prosper and be in health, even as thy soul prospereth."*

He wants His children blessed in every area of their lives. God bestowed blessings upon Abraham, the patriarch of faith. In Genesis 12:1-2, the Lord called Abraham out of his country, kindred and father's house unto an unknown place and God promised to bless him and to make his name great and to make him a blessing. God is a faithful God, He keeps His promises unto a thousand generations, whateve He says He will do that is what He will do, He is a covenant keeping God. He does not lie. Abraham had challenges o life but he overcame every obstacle that came his way. Th bible says in Genesis 13:2, *"And Abram was very rich in cattle, in silver, and in gold."*

Abraham in his days was a great man because the blessing of God was upon him. The word of God says that Abraham was old and well stricken in years and the Lord has blessed him in all things. (Genesis 24:1). The God of Abraham is still God today, He is the same God yesterday, today and forever. He blessed Abraham, He is still blessing today and forever.

Not alone was Abraham blessed, but so was his son Isaac. He was very great. In Genesis 26, the bible says that Isaac was in Gerar where there was a great famine. He wanted to relocate to Egypt but the Lord appeared to him and told him not to and God promised to bless him. He obeyed and stayed in Gerar and the bible says that he sowed in the same land and that same year he reaped a hundredfold. The bible says, " and the Lord bless him." (Genesis 26:13). Isaac was so blessed that the bible says,

13 *"the man waxed great, and went forward and grew un-*

til he became very great: [14] For he had possession of flocks, and possession of herds, and great store of servants: and the Philistines envied him."

Our God is the God of blessings. I pray for you today that the God of blessings will touch your life, in Jesus name. I see you being blessed and being a blessing to your world, in Jesus name. Never underestimate the power of God to bless your life and family. He is the same God yesterday, today and forever, He blessed yesterday, He will bless today and forever. Look up to the only God who can bless abundantly. He is able to do abundantly, above all that we can ask or think according to the power that works in us.

Also, Jacob, Abraham's grandson was not left out of blessings from God. Jacob, the son of Isaac and Rebekah, was sent to his uncle Laban's house in Haran Padan-aram by his mother to escape his brother Esau's wrath. Jacob had tricked his father into giving him the blessing that was meant for Esau. When Jacob was on his way to Padan-aram to live with his uncle Laban, he had a dream and the Lord promised to keep and blessed him. (Genesis 28:10-15). After Jacob arrived at his uncle Laban's house in Haran, he fell in love with Laban's daughter Rachel and agreed to work for Laban for seven years in exchange for her hand in marriage. However, on the wedding day, Laban tricked Jacob and gave him Leah instead of Rachel. Jacob then agreed to work for Laban for another seven years in exchange for Rachel's hand in marriage. (Genesis 29:14-30). During this time, Jacob worked as a shepherd for Laban and was responsible for taking care of his flocks. He made a deal with Laban that he would take all the speckled and spotted sheep and goats as his wages. Laban agreed, but then tried to cheat Jacob by removing all the speckled and spotted animals from the flock. However, with the help of God, Jacob was able to use his knowledge of animal husbandry to breed a large number of speckled and spotted animals, which made him very wealthy. (Genesis:30:25-43). This story teaches us that hard work and perseverance can lead to success, even in the face of adversity with the help of God's blessings.

Jacob was with his uncle for twenty one years where he worked tirelessly. Thank God for the faithfulness of God, Laban tried everything to render Jacob unfruitful but nothing can hinder God's blessing on a life. When Jacob was leaving Laban in Genesis 31:41-42, Jacob said to Laban,

"41 Thus have I been twenty years in thy house; I served thee fourteen years for thy two daughters, and six years for thy cattle: and thou hast changed my wages ten times.

42 Except the God of my father, the God of Abraham, and the fear of Isaac, had been with me, surely thou hadst sent me away now empty. God hath seen mine affliction and the labour of my hands, and rebuked thee yesternight."

God is too faithful to fail; whatever He says He will do, that is what He will do.Jacob was exceedingly great because of the blessings of God upon his life. It was recorded in Genesis 30:43,

“ 43 And the man increased exceedingly, and had much cattle, and maidservants, and menservants, and camels, and asses.”

Abraham was great, Isaac was very great and Jacob was exceedingly great.

You are born to be blessed. That is the reason the bible says n Genesis 1:28, *“And God blessed them, and God said unto them, Be fruitful, and multiply, and replenish the earth, and subdue it: and have dominion over the fish of the sea, and over the fowl of the air, and over every living thing that moveth upon the earth.”*

Never doubt God’s blessing upon your life. The God of blessing is our God. He sent Jesus His son to die for mankind and the bible says that Jesus was made poor so that we can be rich. (2 Corinthians 8:9). Do not settle for less. God wants you to be blessed.

f there is anything or any power working against the blessings of God in your life, I come against them in the name of Jesus. I see the blessing of God locating you. You are moving higher in Jesus' name. I declare you unstoppable. As from today begin to see yourself as a blessed child of God. You will not only be blessed but you will be a blessing to you world, in Jesus name.

CHAPTER 04

GOD IS ABLE TO DELIVER

To deliver simply means to save someone from a painful or bad experience. In the journey of life everyone will encounter one problem or the other. No one is exempted, having troubles or challenges in life is part of living. God knows that man will face challenges in life and that is why the bible says, in Isaiah 43:1-2,

"[1] But now thus saith the Lord that created thee, O Jacob, and he that formed thee, O Israel, Fear not: for I have redeemed thee, I have called thee by thy name; thou art mine. [2] When thou passest through the waters, I will be with thee; and through the rivers, they shall not overflow thee: when thou walkest through the fire, thou shalt not be burned; neither shall the flame kindle upon thee."

Whatever you are going through or is challenging your faith, do not be discouraged, God is very aware of your circumstances and that is why the word of God says when you go through issues of life, He knows and He is the only one that can deliver and He will deliver you. Psalms 50:15 declares; *"And call upon me in the day of trouble: I will deliver thee, and thou shalt glorify me."*

Are you going through any issues in life? Are you afflicted in any way? Are you going through a time of sorrow? Are you being oppressed by the enemy? Are you in any trouble? Do not be discouraged, there is hope for you. God will never abandon you. He will never leave you nor forsake you. Call upon the Lord today. You and I cannot deliver ourselves, only the Lord is powerful enough to deliver from all challenges of life.

In the bible, people of old went through challenges of life, they cried unto the Lord, He answered them. The Lord is the same God yesterday, today and forever, He still answers prayers. He is more than able to deliver His children. I want you to be rest assured that the mighty God is able to deliver you at all times.

Let us look into the examples of people that got into serious problems in the bible and how The Lord delivered them.

1. The three Hebrew men

In Daniel Chapter 3, king Nebuchadnezzar of Babylon made a golden statue and sent messages to all the officials of his provinces to come for the dedication of his golden statue. During the inauguration an herald shouted and told everyone present to bow down to worship the king Nebuchadnezzar's golden image at the sound of the music and whosoever will not obey will immediately be thrown into a blazing furnace. Everyone bowed with the exception of the three Hebrew men, Shedrach, Meshach, and Abed-nego who refused to serve the king's gods nor worship the golden statue that was set up.They were reported to the

King for refusing to bow. The King was very furious and he ordered them to go and bow to his golden image or otherwise he would throw them into the blazing furnace and no one would be able to deliver them from his hands. King Nebuchadnezzar had forgotten that there is a God in Heaven, who is called the mighty deliverer, The King of all kings and The Lord of all lords.

The three Hebrew men told Nebuchadnezzar that the God whom they serve was able to deliver them from the fiery burning furnace and out of his hand. They made it clear to the King that they would never bow to any strange god no matter what. Whoa! What a strong faith in the living God. They stood their ground that they will only worship the living God. As children of the most High God, we must always stand for the Lord.

Are you standing for the Lord?

The bible says that Nebuchadnezzar was very furious and he commanded that the furnace be heated seven times hotter than usual. He commanded the three Hebrew men to be tied up and be thrown into the blazing furnace and because the fire was so hot the bible says that the soldiers that threw the three men were killed by the flames of the fire.

God is the mighty deliver. His word declares, "…..I will deliver you" (Psalms 150:15). The mighty deliver, the Almighty God opened Nebuchadnezzar's eyes, he saw the three Hebrew men, unbound working around in the fire unharmed with the fourth man, walking in the fire.

Daniel 3:26-29, says: "[26] *Then Nebuchadnezzar went near*
the [f]mouth of the burning fiery furnace and spoke, say-
ing, "Shadrach, Meshach, and Abed-Nego, servants of the
Most High God, come out, and come here." Then Shadrach,
Meshach, and Abed-Nego came from the midst of the fire. [27]
And the satraps, administrators, governors, and the king's
counsellors gathered together, and they saw these men on
whose bodies the fire had no power; the hair of their head
was not signed nor were their garments affected, and the
smell of fire was not on them.

[28] *Nebuchadnezzar spoke, saying, "Blessed be the God of*
Shadrach, Meshach, and Abed-Nego, who sent His Angel
and delivered His servants who trusted in Him, and they
have frustrated the king's word, and yielded their bodies
that they should not serve nor worship any god except
their own God! [29] *Therefore I make a decree that any*
people, nation, or language which speaks anything amiss
against the God of Shadrach, Meshach, and Abed-Nego
shall be cut in pieces, and their houses shall be made an
ash heap; because there is no other God who can deliver
like this."

Beloved of God, God delivered the three Hebrew men from the fury furnace. The God of the three Hebrew men is still God yesterday, today, and forever. What do you need to be delivered from? God is well able to deliver you from every issue of life, call upon Him now. His word declares in Psalms 50:15 that we should call upon Him in the day of trouble, He promised to deliver us and we shall glorify Him.

Proverbs 29:25 declares: *"The fear of man brings a snare, But whoever trusts in the LORD shall be safe."*

Call upon Him today!

I see the mighty hand of God delivering you from every

problem, in Jesus name.

2. Daniel

The bible says in Daniel Chapter six that Daniel was more capable than all the other two administrators and high officers that were appointed by king Darius to supervise the 120 provinces in Babylon. The King planned to place Daniel over the entire empire because an excellent spirit was found in him. The bible says the other administrators and high officers were looking for a way to criticise or find a fault in Daniel but they could find none because he was a faithful man and no error was found in him. The administrators and the high officers conspired against Daniel and went to tell the King that all the administrators and high officials had concluded that no one should ask anything from any God apart from the king for 30 days. They convinced the king to sign a decree that whoever will pray to any God apart from the king should be thrown into the lion's den. The king signed the decree. Daniel was a faithful man. The bible says, he prayed three times a day to the mighty God, the God of Abraham, Isaac and Jacob that answers prayers. His enemies who knew that Daniel would certainly pray to His God, saw him praying and reported him to the king. The bible says that when Daniel's report got to the king, the king was very sad because he realised that he could not change the decree he made. The bible says the king was deeply troubled but he did not have a choice than to arrest Daniel and threw him into the lion's den.

Daniel 6:16 says: *"So the king gave the command, and they brought Daniel and cast him into the den of lions. But the king spoke, saying to Daniel, "Your God, whom you serve continually, He will deliver you."*

Watch what the king declared. He said " your God whom you serve continually, will deliver you." (Daniel 6;16). He realised, the God of Daniel is a deliverer.

Do you know that God is the deliverer?

The bible says, the king could not sleep all night and early in the morning according to Daniel 6:20-21 the word of God says, *"[20] And when he came to the den, he cried out with a lamenting voice to Daniel. The king spoke, saying to Daniel, "Daniel, servant of the living God, has your God, whom you serve continually, been able to deliver you from the lions?" [21] Then Daniel said to the king, "O king, live forever! [22] My God sent His angel and shut the lions' mouths, so that they have not hurt me, because I was found innocent before Him; and also, O king, I have done no wrong before you."*

The king was overjoyed and ordered Daniel to be lifted out of the den. There was no scratch found on him. What a mighty God we serve. God delivered Daniel in a miraculous way by shutting the mouth of the lions and they were not able to do Daniel any harm. He was delivered from the wickedness and the conspiracy of the wicked. Glory be to God. Beloved of God, you will not die in your challenges. God will surely deliver you.

Do not doubt Him, He is more than able. The God that delivered Daniel is God the deliverer today and forever, He will surely deliver you from every attack from the pit of hell in the mighty name of Jesus.

I see you being delivered from every power militating against you, in Jesus name.

3. PAUL AND SILAS

In Acts Chapter 16 the bible says that the multitude rose up against Paul and Silas and the magistrates rented off their clothes and ordered that they should be beaten for preaching the Gospel of the Lord Jesus Christ. They were severely beaten with rods and they were put in prison. The bible says they were put in the inner prison and their feet were fastened in an agonising position.

Despite Paul and Silas' ordeal, the bible says, at midnight they prayed and sang praises to the Lord that even other ɔrisoners heard them. And suddenly, there was a great ɘarthquake that was so powerful, it shook the foundation ɔf the prison which opened the prison door and everyone's :hain fell over. The mighty deliverer sent an earthquake, ?aul and Silas were set free. Hallelujah.

Can you pray and praise the Lord? If your answer is yes, I see you coming out of every bondage that has been holding you down. Every captivity over your life is breaking now in esus name.

ames 5:13 says, *"Is anyone among you suffering? Let him ɔray. Is anyone cheerful? Let him sing psalms."*

Pray and praise, God who watches over His word will surely leliver you. God is able to deliver you. Psalms 50:15 says, *'Call upon me in the day of trouble, I will deliver you and thou shall glorify me."*

here is no problem that is above the name of Jesus. At the ıame of Jesus, every knee must bow.

here is power in that name. There is deliverance in that

name. Call upon the name JESUS now.

This is your day of deliverance. Whatever has been holding you down, be free now in Jesus name. Praise the Lord for your freedom.

CHAPTER 05

GOD IS ABLE TO KEEP YOU.

No man can keep himself totally secured, only God the Almighty can keep anyone. He is the keeper and sustainer of all. No one is fully secured without the Lord. He is the one that neither sleeps nor slumber and He keeps watch over His children twenty four seven.

Psalms 121:3-8 says; *"3 He will not allow your foot to be moved; He who keeps you will not slumber. 4 Behold, He who keeps Israel Shall neither slumber nor sleep. 5 The Lord is your keeper; The Lord is your shade at your right hand. 6 The sun shall not strike you by day, Nor the moon by night. 7 The Lord shall preserve you from all evil; He shall preserve your soul. 8 The Lord shall preserve your going out and your coming in From this time forth, and even forevermore."*

Your security and mine is in the Lord. He is able to keep us from all situations that can hamper our destiny. He is our keeper and refuge.

Psalms 91:9-14 says,"9 *Because you have made the Lord,*
who is my refuge, Even the Most High, your dwelling
place, 10 *No evil shall befall you, Nor shall any plague come*
near your dwelling; 11 *For He shall give His angels charge*
over you, To keep you in all your ways. 12 *In their hands*
they shall bear you up, Lest you dash your foot against a
stone. 13 *You shall tread upon the lion and the cobra, The*
young lion and the serpent you shall trample underfoot.
14 *"Because he has set his love upon Me, therefore I will*
deliver him;"

Whatever you pledge to God, He can keep: your life, marriage, children, health, business, career, etc. He has the capacity to hold us through. What is entrusted to God can be maintained by Him alone.

Have you entrusted your life unto Him?

Is He in charge of your life?

Is your totality on Him?

God is more than capable to keep all that is committed into His hands. He is well able to sustain your life and mine.

He is the only one that will never mismanage our lives. The God that watches over us does not slumber nor sleep. His love for us is unmeasurable.

Let us look at some examples of those God kept in the Bible.

1. God kept Moses.

In Exodus chapter 1, Pharaoh, the king of Egypt ordered the midwives to throw every newborn boy that was born by the Hebrew women in the land of Egypt into the Nile River. Exodus chapter 2 recorded that Moses was born to Jocobed and Amram. Amiram kept the baby hidden for three months because she saw that the child was a special baby. At one point she could not hide the baby anymore so she made a basket and put the baby in it and she laid it among the reeds along the bank of the Nile River and told

Miriam the baby's sister to watch from a distance to see what will happen to the baby.

God is the master planner. He knows all things and He will do all things. God brought Pharaoh's daughter at the right time to come to the Nile for a bath and she noticed the basket that the baby was in. She opened it and saw the little Hebrew baby boy crying and the bible says, the princess felt sorry for the baby. Immediately, Miriam who was watching from a distance showed up and asked the princess if she could get her a nurse and she accepted. The princess named the baby, Moses, she said because she drew him out of the water. Moses' mother was paid by the princess to nurse her own baby. What a mighty God we serve.

God is the one that keeps. Truly, He watches over His own. Imagine this, God did not allow the wave of the river to carry away the baby with the basket. He did not allow the scorpion to sting the baby. God allowed the princess to locate baby Moses. What a marvellous God we serve. He is Able to Keep His own. His keeping you is guaranteed.

2 Timothy 1:12 declares; *"…for I know whom I have believed, and am persuaded that he is able to keep that which I have committed unto him against that day."*

Commit everything to Jesus today, do not hold back anything. Whatever it is, commit it to Him. He is well able to keep you.

2. God kept David from Saul

The children of Israel demanded for a king in 1 Samuel chapter 8 and in Samuel chapter 9, Saul was chosen to be king of Israel and in 1 Samuel chapter 10, he was anointed the king of Israel. During the reign of king Saul, the Lord instructed him through prophet Samuel to carry out an assignment in 1 Samuel 15: 1-3. *"Samuel also said unto Saul, The Lord sent me to anoint thee to be king over his people, over Israel: now therefore hearken thou unto the voice of the words of the Lord. [2]Thus saith the Lord of hosts, I re member that which Amalek did to Israel, how he laid wai for him in the way, when he came up from Egypt.[3] Now g and smite Amalek, and utterly destroy all that they hav and spare them not; but slay both man and woman, infan and suckling, ox and sheep, camel and ass."*

During the reign of king Saul in 1 Samuel 15. Saul went a he was instructed but he did not obey God fully. God saic destroy the Amalekites completely but Saul spared Agag th king, the best of the sheep, oxen and lambs that was gooc (1 Samuel 15:9).

What Saul did made the Lord to reject Saul as king and Da vid was chosen in his place to be the king of Israel and in Samuel chapter 16 David was anointed by Prophet Samue as the king of Israel. The bible says, *"that the spirit of th Lord departed from king Saul and an evil spirit from th Lord troubled him." (1 Samuel 16:14).*

Saul was advised by his servants to look for a man who ca play a harp so that when the music was being played, h would be well. David who was skillful in playing the har was introduced to king Saul and anytime the evil spirit will come upon Saul, David played the harp for him and the bible says Saul was refreshed and well and the evil spirit departed from him. (1 Samuel 16:14-23).

In 1 Samuel chapter 17 the bible recorded that the Philistines came against Israel for battle and Goliath, Philistine champion from Gath, challenged Israel to choose someone from the ranks of Israel to fight him. The bible says when the children of Israel heard the words of the Philistine, they were very afraid. For 40 days Goliath threatened the army of Israel but no one was able to come out and face Goliath. Jesse David's father sent David to go and give food to his brothers at the battle field. When he got there he saw how Goliath was defiling the God of Israel and calling the Israel army to select a champion to fight him. David made the decision to take on Goliath.The bible says in 1 Samuel 17:50; *" So David prevailed over the Philistine with a sling and with a stone, and smote the Philistine, and slew him; but there was no sword in the hand of David."*

From the day David defeated Goliath, the bible says that Saul became jealous of David because when David defeated Goliath the bible says that when the women came dancing before Saul because of the victory over the Philistines , they began to sing "Saul slain his thousands, and

David his ten thousands." King Saul was very angry because he said the people ascribed thousands to him and ten thousands to David and he eyed David from that day forward. (1 Samuel 1:9).

Afterward, the bible says the evil spirit came upon king Saul and David played the harp for him but Saul had his javelin in his hand and he tried to pin David to the wall twice but God kept David.

I pray for you that the Lord will keep you from your enemies. God will not allow the plans of the enemy to prevail.

Saul wanted David dead but the Lord preserved David's life. King Saul gave his daughter Micah to David to marry and he said David should not worry about dowry but instead David should give him a hundred foreskins of the Philistines. Saul's intention was for David to fall by the hand of the Philistines. David went to the camp of the Philistines and slew 200 hundred men and he brought back their foreskins and gave them to the king. He became king Saul's in law.

The bible says Saul saw and knew that the Lord was with David. Saul became afraid of David and became David's enemy continually. Despite all the mischievous behaviour of Saul, The Lord of Israel kept David.

At a point, Saul even told Jonathan his son and other people in 1 Samuel 19 to kill David. The bible says Jonathan delighted in David and he tried to speak good about David to his father and Saul promised not to kill David. Despite Jonathan's efforts to save David from the father, Saul intended to kill David. The bible says Jonathan brought David before Saul and again Saul tried to pin David to the wall with his javelin while playing the harp for Saul. David escaped again. The Lord again saved David from Saul's evil intentions.

Saul's malicious intentions persisted. The exact night when Saul dispatched messengers to David's home to kill him, David's wife Micah gave him the signal to flee and let him through a window in a basket. David got away once more. The bible says the Lord is our keeper and our shield. (Psalms 121:5).

Throughout the reign of King Saul, he was always pursuing David but the keeper of Israel did not allow the evil intentions of Saul to come to pass. In 1 Samuel 24 it was recorded that Saul took 3,000 men to seek after David but God kept David from evil. Also, in 1 Samuel 26, Saul took another 3000 men to destroy David but again, God did not allow the will of Saul to come to pass. David had to escape to the land of the Philistines to rest from king Saul. (1 Samuel 27). In the end through the help of God David was preserved by God and Saul died.

The bible says, in 2 Samuel 3:1, *" Now there was long war between the house of Saul and the house of David: but David waxed stronger and stronger, and the house of Saul waxed weaker and weaker."*

What a mighty God we serve. He is the one that keeps His children. The same God that saved David from Saul.

He is alive for evermore and He will always keep His own children. Always remember that the Lord is your keeper and there is nothing to be afraid of. God is able to keep to the end.

3. God kept Joseph

The account of Joseph in the book of Genesis 37, 39-4 serves as one illustration of how God protects someon from evil. Joseph's siblings hated him because he was love by Jacob, their father and because Joseph was a dream er. They sold him as a slave to the Amalekites and th Amalekites took Joseph captive into Egypt and Joseph wa sold to Potiphar, an officer of Pharaoh. Potiphar's wif lied against Joseph and he was thereafter held captive fo a crime he didn't commit. But despite all of his hardship God was with him, and he ultimately rose to become th second-most powerful man in Egypt.

Joseph pardoned his brothers and stated, *"You intende to harm me, but God intended it for good to accomplis what is now being done, the saving of many lives,"* whe they travelled to Egypt during a famine in search of foo (Genesis 50:20).

Looking at the life of Joseph the Lord kept him all the way and he was able to fulfil his destiny. No matter what you are passing through, l have good news for you, the Lord will surely keep you and you shall fulfil your destiny in Jesus name. There is a greater tomorrow ahead of you. The best is yet to come.

CHAPTER 06

GOD IS ABLE TO KEEP YOU FROM FALLING.

Only the Lord is able to sustain us. He is the Lord that has the power and the might that can keep us from falling. In the journey of life there are many pit holes, but God is capable of keeping us from every visible and invisible pit. Jude 1:24-25 says, "[24] *Now to Him who is able to keep you from stumbling, And to present you faultless Before the presence of His glory with exceeding joy,* [25] *To God our Saviour, Who alone is wise, Be glory and majesty, Dominion and power, Both now and forever. Amen."*

In life there are different kinds of pits that only God can deliver one from. No one desires to fall but life is like a roller coaster. Falling into pits can be likened to falling into problems and problems of life differ. Health issues, financial troubles, infertility, unemployment, lack, business failure, marital issues, temptations, etc. are some of the issues that people face. Falling into any one of these issues is like falling into a pit. All thanks be to God who is able to rescue us and keep us from falling. God is ever-present to support us and prevent us from falling. For His children, this provides consolation and hope. I decree and declare any pit of challenges that you are struggling with, come out in the mighty name of Jesus. No power of hell can keep you in the pit. Any demon trying to keep you in the pit, the powers are scattered in the name of Jesus and consumed by the fire of the Holy Ghost, our God is a consuming fire.

Looking through the bible there are many examples of those that God delivered from problems both in the New and the Old Testament. The Bible contains many stories of people who got into problems that were meant to destroy them and God delivered them. The Lord did not promise us a problem free life, His word in Isaiah 43:1 says " *When ye pass through .....*" The bible did not say if you pass through. This means that as human beings we are bound to go through one issue or the other. Everyone will go through something, it is just that nobody knows when. One thing that is certain is that God is able to keep us from falling, that is, God is able to sustain no matter the situation. The word of declares in

Psalms 91:1-6:" [1] *He who dwells in the secret place of the Most High Shall abide under the shadow of the Almighty.* [2] *I will say of the LORD, "He is my refuge and my fortress; My God, in Him I will trust."* [3] *Surely He shall deliver you from the snare of the fowler And from the perilous pestilence.* [4] *He shall cover you with His feathers, And under His wings you shall take refuge; His truth shall be your shield and buckler.* [5] *You shall not be afraid of the terror by night, Nor of the arrow that flies by day,* [6] *Nor of the pestilence that walks in darkness, Nor of the destruction that lays waste at noonday."*

Dwelling under the shadow of the Almighty guarantees a

believer's safety, no power of darkness can overcome the children of the most High God.

These are some of the examples of those who encountered problems in the journey of life and were kept by God:

1. Children of Israel in the wilderness

The remarkable story of God's grace and provision for the Israelites in the wilderness is recorded in the book of Exodus. It recounts how God delivered the Israelites from slavery in Egypt. For forty years after departing from Egypt, the Israelites wandered in the wilderness. The children of Israel encountered a number of difficulties while travelling across the wilderness during this time but the Lord sustained them. Here are some of the challenges they faced:

I. Fear and uncertainty: When the children of Israel left

Egypt after 430 years of being in Egypt, they were afraid o: the Egyptians who were chasing them, and the Israelites did not know what was ahead of them because of the rec sea. (Exodus 14:5-10).

II. Lack of water and food. The children of lsrael com plained about lack of water and food in the wilderness bu God made water to flow from the rock to quench thei thirst and rained manna from heaven to feed them. (Exodu: 15:22-26 and Exodus 16:1-23).

III. Hostile nations: The children of lsrael encounterec unfriendly nations such as the Amalekites who attackec them but lsrael was victorious. (Exodus 17:8-16).

IV. Harsh weather conditions: Extreme heat and colc were among the terrible weather conditions that the Israe ites had to face but God sustained them. The bible says tha their clothes and shoes did not wear out. (Nehemiah 9:21

God met the needs of the Israelites and guided them through the wilderness in spite of these difficulties.The biblical account of the Israelites in the barren wilderness serves as a proof of God's faithfulness and kindness.

2. Jonah in the Belly of the Whale

One of the most famous biblical stories is the one about Jonah and the whale in the book of Jonah. The Bible states that Jonah was a prophet who attempted to escape on a ship after refusing to preach to the Ninevites at the behest of God. In order to placate God's wrath, the sailors throw Jonah overboard when he sent a powerful storm that threatened to wreck the ship.

After that, Jonah was swallowed by a large fish—some refer to it as a whale—and lived inside of it for three days and three nights. Jonah confessed his sins, praised God, and pleaded to God for assistance during this time. The Lord who is able to keep, sustained Jonah alive for 3 days in the belly of the whale. God gave the fish the order to spew Jonah out upon Nineveh's shores. Following Jonah's sermon, the Ninevites turned from their sins. Jonah's encounter with the whale serves as a potent reminder of God's sustainability, kindness, and grace.

3. Peter kept from the evil plan of Herod

In Acts 12:1-12 King Herod began to persecute the Church and executed James, the brother of John. He then arrested Peter during the Feast of Unleavened Bread, intending to bring him to trial after Passover. Peter was kept in prison, but the Church prayed fervently for him. On the eve of Peter's trial, an angel of the Lord woke him, freeing him from his chains and led him out of the prison. Peter initially thought he was dreaming, but upon realising his freedom, he acknowledged it as the Lord's doing. The Lord kept him from the evil desire of Herod. Peter went to Mary's house, where many believers had gathered to pray. A servant girl named Rhoda recognized Peter's voice at the gate but left him outside in her excitement. Eventually, Peter was let in and recounted his miraculous escape, asking them to relay the news to James and the brothers.

These stories are a testament to God's power and love for his people. They remind us that no matter what problems we face, God is always there to help His children. He is our keeper, always keeping His children because of His love for us.

CHAPTER 07

GOD IS ABLE TO MAKE A WAY.

The Lord Almighty is the way maker. He is able to make a way where there is no way.

Isaiah 43:19 says, " *Behold, I will do a new thing; now it shall spring forth; shall ye not know it? I will even make a way in the wilderness, and rivers in the desert.*"

Before God, the phrase "road block" does not exist. God is able to make a way where man will conclude there is no way. He is the way. John 14: 6 declares Jesus is the way the truth and the life. He knows the way because He is called the Alpha and the Omega, the Beginning and the End, the First and the Last. Nothing is hidden from Him. The bible says, in Psalms 23:2b that *"…He leads me through the path of righteousness for His name sake…."*

In the word of God there are many examples of God making a way for His children because He delight in making a way where there is no way. One of the greatest examples of God making a way for His children is the story of the children of Israel by the Red Sea in Exodus 14.

God made a way for the children of Israel when they came out of the land of Egypt. The bible says God brought the children of Israel out of Egypt by a mighty hand. (Exodus 12:51). The children of Israel were glad to be out of slavery in the land of Egypt under Pharaoh.

The bible says in Exodus 14 that Pharaoh the king of Egypt heard the news that the Israelites had fled from Egypt, Pharaoh and his men pursued after the children of Israel. The Israelites were sorely afraid when they saw Pharaoh approaching them. They cried out against Moses asking him if there were no graves in Egypt. To make matters worse the Egyptians were pursuing Israel and the Red Sea was in front of them. Moses told the people to be still and that the Egyptians they see today, they shall see them no more because the Lord will fight for them. I guess the people would ask Moses,

"Do you know what you are saying?

Are you realistic at all?

Can't you see the red sea?

How are we going to cross the red sea?

Moses told the people to stay calm and not be afraid and see the Lord rescued them from the Egyptians because the Egyptians they saw that day, they will never see again (Exodus:14:13).

The Lord is telling you today, be calm and stop being afraid because the Lord will make a way for you where there is no way. Whatever represents Pharaoh or Red Sea in your life, the mighty surely deliver you and make a way for you.

He is the mighty deliverer that makes a way where there is no way.

The Lord told Moses, tell the people to get moving. In other words, stop panicking, move forward. God told Moses to raise his rod towards the Red Sea and Moses did and the Red Sea parted and the children of Israel walked on dry ground. What a mighty God we serve. The ocean divider turned the Red Sea into an express way for the children of Israel to go through. The Egyptians tried to follow the children of Israel into the dry Red Sea but the Egyptians were destroyed in the Red Sea because theLord Almighty closed the Red Sea on the Egyptians.

The bible says in Exodus Chapter 14:30-31, *"30 Thus the Lord saved Israel that day out of the hand of the Egyptians; and Israel saw the Egyptians dead upon the sea shore. 31 And Israel saw that great work which the Lord did upon the Egyptians: and the people feared the Lord, and believed the Lord, and his servant Moses."*

Beloved of God, the same God that made a way for the children of Israel is the same God yesterday, today and forever. He made a way for the children of Israel, He will also make a way for you too.

In which areas of your life are you believing God to make ways for you?

He is more than able. The bible says He is able to do exceedingly, abundantly above all that we can ask from Him. (Ephesians 3:19).

God will surely make a way for you. Be rest assured, He is well able. Just put your trust in the living God, He does not disappoint, and He will never let you down. I see the mighty hand of God making a way for you where there is no way. Never think you are at the end of the road, the Lord will surely make a way for you out of that difficult situation.

He is God from the beginning to the end and He is the way maker.

Whatever stands as an obstacle in your life is being removed right now in Jesus name. Every power of darkness from your father's house, mother' house, in law's house or from anywhere standing as an obstacle are scattered by thunder from above in Jesus name.

The word of God will never fail, He promised to make a way in the wilderness and flowing waters in the desert place. He will pave a way where there is no way. I see God doing new things in your life. It is a new beginning in your life. Your season of blocked ways is over from now.

Shout it out loud, "IT IS A NEW DAY FOR ME. MY GOD IS MAKING A WAY FOR ME. ALLELUYAH."

CHAPTER 08

GOD IS ABLE TO BRING BACK TO LIFE.

God is the giver of life because He is life. The Bible frequently discusses God's ability to revive the dead.

Psalms 30:3 says,
"O LORD, You brought my soul up from the grave;

You have kept me alive, that I should not go down to the pit."

Only God by His power brings back the dead. Just as He alone is able to preserve and restore life. He is called the resurrection and the life. Exploring through the bible there are diverse examples of cases of those who died and the power of God brought them back to life both in the Old and the New Testament.

Here are a few Old Testament examples

1. The son of the widow of Zarephath:

In 1 Kings 17:17-24, the prophet Elijah the Tishbite had been staying at a widow's home in Zarephath, a heathen city in Phoenicia, during a period of severe drought. The woman's son became ill without warning and eventually ceased breathing. For the boy's life to return, Elijah prayed to God, who promised to answer our prayers when we call upon Him in faith. Elijah's prayers were answered by God, the restorer and the child came back to life. God is the same God yesterday, today and forever. The same God that restored the dead boy's life is still restoring lives today. God answered prayers yesterday, He will answer today, and forever. The same God that answered the prayers of Elijah still answers prayers. God is able to touch every dead situation. As a believer, what we need to do is call upon God in every situation. The bible says call upon God on the day of trouble He will answer us and deliver us. Is there any situation you are passing through and it looks like a dead situation, cry out to God in prayers, He will answer you, He will never fail you.

2. **Son of the Shunammite Woman**

The bible says in 2 Kings 4:18-37 that prophet Elisha resid ed in the upper chamber of a prosperous Shunem couple Elisha prayed that God would grant the couple a child because they did not have a child. God heard his praye and the couple had a son. After a few years, the boy died after complaining of a headache. Mouth to mouth, eyes to eyes, hands to hands, Elisha laid himself on the lifeless body, calling out to the Lord. As his body warmed up, the boy sneezed seven times, and then he opened his eyes. Th Almighty, the restorer of life, restored the dead boy. What a mighty God we serve. All things are possible to those that believe and call upon the living God.

3. Israelite Man:

In 2 Kings 13:20-21, the bible recorded that Prophet Elisha was buried in a tomb after his death. Every spring, Israel was attacked by the Moabite raiders, who broke up a burial procession . Elisha's grave was the first convenient site the burial party hurriedly placed the body into out of fear for their own lives. The deceased man reanimated and rose up as soon as the corpse made contact with Elisha's bones. The resurrection and the life gave breath of life to the dead body.

Examples from the New Testament

The resurrection power that worked in the Old Testament, operated also in the New Testament because the Old Testament is a shadow of the New Testament.The power of God is always available for His people if only we can believe His unfailing words. Let us explore some of the examples of those who died and came back to life.

1. **Lazarus:**

Lazarus, a resident of Bethany, became gravely ill in John Chapter 11, and his sisters, Mary and Martha, informed Jesus, pleading with him,

"Lord, the one you love is sick." Jesus answered, "There will be no death from this illness. No, it is for the glory of God, so that God's Son may be exalted in it. Jesus purposefully stayed back for four days despite the urgency. Lazarus had already been buried for four days and the body was already decomposing when Jesus finally made it to Bethany. "My brother would not have died if you had been here," Martha sobbed when she first saw Jesus. Jesus declared, "I am the resurrection and the life,"

(John 11:25). Jesus gave her the assurance that her brother would rise again. Jesus wept and He asked for where Lazarous was laid and told them to roll away the stone covering Lazarus tomb. Martha, Lazarous' sister, told Jesus that Lazarous had been dead for 4 days and the body was already stinking. Jesus told Martha that if she would believe she would see the glory of the Lord. Jesus looked up to Heaven and gave thanks to God for always hearing Him and cried out in a loud voice, "Lazarous come forth." And the bible says Lazarous that was dead came forth miraculously, bound in grave cloth. The power of God moved upon the decomposed body of Lazarous and life of God entered into him. Jesus said, lose him and let him go. Lazarous was untied from the grave cloth. Jesus boldly declared, "Did I not tell you that if you believe you would see the glory of God?"

The significance of Lazarus's resurrection lies in the fact that it showed how powerful Jesus is over death. Jesus is the resurrection and the life. This account demonstrates God's ability to raise the dead. They serve as a reminder that there is always hope for a better tomorrow, even in the most dire circumstances of life.

2. The Widow of Nain

Jesus, together with His disciples and a large crowd, reportedly travelled to the town of Nain, according to the Gospel of Luke, chapter 7:1. There was a funeral procession going on as He got closer to the town gate. The dead person was a widow's only son. She was devastated not only because she had lost her but she was hopeless being a widow. Jesus had compassion for the bereaved widow when He saw her. Jesus told her to stop crying. Jesus went over to the platform holding the body on a bier and touched it. Speaking to the youth directly, *"Young man, I say to you, get up!"* he commanded. The dead man miraculously sat up and started talking. He was raised to life by Jesus, who then gave him back to his mother. The crowd were overwhelmed with astonishment and awe. The words *"God has come to help His people"* resounded in their declaration. (Luke 7:11-17) Word of this remarkable event quickly travelled throughout Judea and the neighbouring areas.The son of the widow became a living example of Jesus' victory over death.

This story serves as a reminder that nothing is insurmountable for God. He has the power to revive people from the brink of death.The widow's story illustrates how having faith in Christ Jesus can lead to the hope of resurrection and eternal life.

3. The raising of Jairus daughter

Jairus, the ruler of a synagogue in Galilee, approaches Jesus in Mark 5:21–43 with a very touching plea. His 12-year-old daughter was very sick and on the verge of passing away. In the gospels of Mark and Luke, Jairus begged Jesus to save or heal his daughter. Mathew 9: 18-26 merely says that she had just passed away and begged Jesus to lay His hand upon her in order for her to be resurrected. Another incident breaks up the story as Jesus followed Jairus to his home because a woman who has been bleeding constantly for 12 years came to Jesus. She thought in her heart that she would be healed if she could simply touch His robe.

Her faith was rewarded when she touched Jesus' coat, which caused her bleeding to stop immediately.While this encounter unfolded, messengers arrived with devastating news for Jairus that his daughter had died. Imagine Jairu anguish as he heard this. His hope for healing had turned into grief. Despite the girl's apparent death, Jesus remained undeterred. He told Jairus, “Do not fear; only believe.” Upon reaching Jairus’ house, Jesus entered the room where the lifeless girl was laid. He took her by the hand and said, “Talithacumi,” which means “Little girl, I say to you, arise.” Miraculously, the girl came back to life! Her spirit returned, and she sat up. The scene was witnessed by Jairus, his wife, and three of Jesus’ disciples—Peter, James, and John. These witnesses attested to the reality of the resurrection. Beyond the physical healing, this miracle revealed a deeper message. It reveals Jesus’ authority over sickness and death. Just as He restored Jairus’ daughter to life, Jesus offers spiritual healing and eternal life to all who believe in Him.

In this extraordinary event, we see the able power of God resurrecting Jairus’ daughter. This serves as a beacon of hope for all who face despair and loss. There is no situation Jehovah God cannot turn around for a miracle.

In conclusion, God's capacity to bring the dead back to life is proof of His mercy and love. It acts as a reminder that, even in the most trying circumstances, there is always hope for a brighter tomorrow.

God is able to bring whatever is dead back to life, He is called the resurrection and the life.

CHAPTER 09

GOD IS ABLE TO SILENCE THE ENEMY.

The power of God is unlimited. He is the great God that has the ability to do great and mighty things. He is able to deal with our enemies.

Deuteronomy 20:3-4 declares:" [3] *And he shall say to them, 'Hear, O Israel: Today you are on the verge of battle with your enemies. Do not let your heart faint, do not be afraid, and do not tremble or be terrified because of them;* [4] *for the LORD your God is He who goes with you, to fight for you against your enemies, to save you."*

What the Lord says to one, He says to all. He is the same God yesterday, today and forever. He fought for the children of lsrael yesterday and today and He is fighting for us too. Whatever is fighting you, you must not be afraid or terrified of the enemies, for the Lord is with you and He is fighting your battles for you. God will surely silence all your enemies.

According to Psalms 143:12, King David said *"In your unfailing love, silence my enemies; destroy all my foes, for I am your servant."*

Throughout the life of king David, the famous king of Israel, encountered many adversaries. He came to the realisation that it was God that could silence all his enemies and bring destruction to his foes. David knew that he could not defeat his enemies by his own power and might because the word of God declares that for by strength shall no man prevail. Let us look into some of King David's enemies that the Lord delivered David from in the bible.

1. **Goliath**

In 1 Samuel Chapter 17, Goliath, a giant from the city of Gath, was the champion of the Philistines. Goliath was a towering figure, standing six cubits and a span (about nine feet nine inches). He had scale armour covering his body, a bronze helmet, and bronze greaves on his legs. The iron tip of his spear, which resembled a weaver's rod, weighed six hundred shekels. He was accompanied by a shield bearer. With a mocking yell, "Why do you come out and queue for battle?" Goliath addressed the ranks of Israelites. Are you not Saul's servants, and am I not a Philistine? Select a male and ask him to come to me.

He declared a duel in which the Philistines would become Israel's subjects if an Israelite defeated him, and the Israelites would serve the Philistines if he prevailed. The bible says Goliath taunted the children of Israel for 40 days and Israel's army were very afraid. No man was willing to confront Goliath.

During this period David was taking care of his father's sheep in Bethlehem. He was the youngest son of Jesse. Goliath challenged the Israelites day and night for forty days but no one was brave enough to confront him. David was dispatched by Jesse to see how his older brothers, who were in Saul's army, were doing. David heard Goliath's daring comments as he drew closer to the battle lines. Inspired by bravery and faith, David offered to take on Goliath.He disregarded conventional armour in favour of a basic sling and stones.

David was made fun of by Goliath, but the young shepherd did not waver. David aimed his sling and hit Goliath in the forehead with just one stone. The unlikely hero had triumphed over the Goliath. David's triumph shows us that despite what seems like insurmountable obstacles, faith tenacity, and inventiveness can triumph. It serves as a re minder that even the most unlikely people are able to defeat their enemies with the help of the Lord of Host. David's win signalled the start of his ascent to fame and demonstrated his steadfast faith in God.

In the journey of life, there are giants that are positioned by the devil to harass people of God, but in the name of Jesus every giant shall be destroyed. The same anointing that destroyed Goliath of Gath is still available to God's children today. Do not allow any giant to intimidate you. You know why? 1 John 4:4b declares, greater is He that is in us than he that is in the world. Hallelujah. I see you walking in victory in the name of Jesus. Glory be to God.

2. **King Saul**

In 1 Samuel Chapter 16:1-13, Prophet Samuel anointed David as the future king over lsrael secretly, Saul persecuted David although Saul was the reigning king. David was pursued relentlessly by king Saul because of jealousy and fear. However, the Lord, the great protector, had His hand of protection on David. He was protected from king Saul's traps and the evil attempts. Every evil agenda against David's life failed because the Lord was with David. The word of God declares, "....*if God be for us who can be against you?* (Romans 8:31). Dear child of God, l see God giving you victory, in the name of Jesus.

Beloved of God, l want you to know that the Lord will not allow stubborn pursuers to overcome you, call upon the Lord today and He will surely deliver you from every enemy of your destiny.

The bible says in Psalms 56:9, *"When I cry out to You, Then my enemies will turn back; This I know, because God is for me."*

If God is for you, who can be against you. No one, because you are born to be victorious. You are born a winner. I see you walking in victory in Jesus name.

3. **Absalom (David's Son):**

In 2 Samuel Chapter 15 there is the account of a dramatic and intriguing Biblical tale of Absalom's rebellion against his father, King David. Known for his remarkable looks and charisma, Absalom was one of King David's sons. Establishing himself as a fair and empathetic judge, he started hatching plans against his father, King David. Absalom would stand by the city entrance, where citizens would come to bring their complaint to king David. He would hear their complaints, and he would express his desires to be their judge instead of king David. As a result of Absalom actions the people began to prefer Absalom over King David as he became more and more popular over time.

Four years later, Absalom asked David for permission to visit Hebron. He said that it was to carry out a promise he had made to the Lord when he was a resident of Geshur. Actually, Absalom took advantage of the occasion to rally support for his uprising. He announced that he was now king of Hebron by sending emissaries in secret to the northern tribes of Israel. David made the decision to depart Jerusalem after learning of Absalom's expanding power in order to escape conflict. He was escorted by his officers and men. As they left the city, David watched his loyal troops march past, including the 600 soldiers who had followed him from Gath.

David watched his faithful army, which followed him from Gath, march by as they departed the city. Ittai, a foreigner who had just lately joined David's army, was one of them. David learned that everyone of Israel was supporting Absalom as he proceeded to garner support. David's officials begged him to leave Jerusalem right away out of fear for their lives. They were aware that they would be in great danger if Absalom found them. Ten of David's wives were left behind to take care of the palace, while the rest of his family and devoted supporters went with him. As Absalom's rebellion grew more intense, a conflict broke out between his army and David's supporters. A horrible end befell Absalom in the ensuing struggle as his hair got tangled in a ree's branches while he was fleeing on a mule.

Before the battle started, David begged Joab, one of his commanders, to spare his son, but Joab found him and killed him. David expressed his profound sadness at the passing of his cherished son as he lamented

Absalom's passing.The narrative of Absalom's uprising functions as a warning against ambition, treachery, and the results of pursuing power at any cost.

Throughout David's trials, he acknowledged God's hand in

his victories. He recognised the Lord as his deliverer and his trust in God's protection and guidance sustained him through adversity.

In summary, David's life was marked by both external enemies and internal struggles, but his faith and reliance on God allowed him to overcome formidable odds and establish a legacy as a man after God's own heart.

CHAPTER 10

GOD IS ABLE TO HEAL.

When God created man in His image and likeness, man was perfect because the bible says that all that God created was good and perfect. God did not create sickness with mankind. When Adam and Eve disobeyed God evil came into the world. It was the wish of God from the beginning for man to enjoy divine health. His words declares in 3 John 2: *"Beloved, I pray that you may prosper in all things and be in health, just as your soul prospers."* Sin came into the world and man started having illnesses but God made provision for man's healing by sending His son Jesus to the cross to die for man. On the cross Jesus said,

"It is finished". In other words every evil against mankind is finished.

The word of God declares in isaiah 53:3-5;*"[3] He is despised and rejected by men, A Man of sorrows and acquainted with grief. And we hid, as it were, our faces from Him; He was despised, and we did not esteem Him. [4] Surely He has borne our griefs And carried our sorrows; Yet we esteemed Him stricken, Smitten by God, and afflicted.[5] But He was wounded for our transgressions, He was bruised for our iniquities; The chastisement for our peace was upon Him, And by His stripes we are healed"*

Scripture abounds in stories and promises of health and healing for God's children in the Bible. God's covenant with the children of Israel reflects His ever-present nature towards us in this regard. "I will put none of these diseases upon thee, which I have brought upon the Egyptians: for I am the Lord that healeth thee," He declares in Exodus 15:26. Also, in Psalm 103:1-3, King David acknowledges that covenant by saying: *"Bless the Lord, O my soul: and all that is within me, bless his holy name. Bless the Lord, O my soul, and forget not all his benefits: Who forgiveth all thine iniquities; who healeth all thy diseases."*

Exploring through the Old and New Testament of the bible there are numerous examples of people that received their healings. The word of God declares in Psalms 107:20 that *"He sent His word and healed them,And delivered them from their destructions."*

The Lord healed yesterday, He is healing today and for evermore. Hallelujah.

Examples of healing from the Old Testament:

1. **Abraham's intercession for Abimelech:**

In Genesis 20:1-18, Abraham and Sarah settled in Gerar while on their way to the Negeb. Abraham, out of fear, pretended that Sarah was his sister and King Abimelech of Gerar took Sarah for himself. There was a divine intervention from Heaven, God warned Abimelech in a dream that he would die if he approached Sarah. Abimelech was instructed by God to return Sarah to Abraham, and God told Abimelech that Abraham would pray for him, for he was a prophet. Abimelech returned Sarah to Abraham and questioned him about the deception. Abraham explained that he feared for his life in this godless place and that Sarah was indeed his half-sister. Abimelech gave riches to Abraham and allowed him to settle wherever he pleased. Abraham prayed to God and God healed Abimelech, his wife and his female servants so that they could have children. God opened the wombs of Abimelech's wife and other household women that were previously closed. God is the healer.

2. Hannah healed from barrenness

The story of Hannah is a touching account of healing from barrenness found in the Biblical book of 1 Samuel. Hannah was one of the two wives of a man named Elkanah. Unfortunately, she was barren and unable to have children

Her rivalry, Peninnah, had children and she would taunt Hannah and make fun of her. Yearly Elkanah would go to Shiloh with his family to worship the Lord. One year Hannah stayed back at Shiloh and prayed a specific, desperate prayer unto the Lord that the Lord should bless her with a male child. While Hannah was pouring out her heart to the Lord, Priest Eli took her for a drunken woman because only Hannah's mouth was moving while she was pouring out her heart to the Lord. Hannah explained that she was praying o the Lord. Eli declared unto Hannah that the God of Israel would grant her request. Hannah returned home with oy and conceived. She gave birth to a boy and she named him Samuel, which means *"I have asked for him from the LORD"* (1 Samuel 1:20). When Samuel was weaned, Hannah and Samuel travelled back to Shiloh. They brought a acrifice to the Lord andHannah presented Samuel to Eli, saying, "I prayed for this child, and the Lord has granted me what I asked. So now I give him to the Lord. For his whole life, he will be dedicated to the Lord.

3. Namaan was healed of leprosy

The story of Naaman in 2 Kings Chapter 5 is an account of a miraculous healing. The bible says in 2 Kings 5:1 that the king of Aram had great admiration for Naaman, who was the commander of his army, because under Naaman, the LORD had given Aram great victories. Although Naaman was a mighty warrior, he was a leper.

A young girl from Israel, who had been captured by Aramean raiders and now served Naaman's wife, encouraged Naaman's wife to tell his husband to go to Samaria to meet prophet Elisha for his healing.

Naaman followed her advice and journeyed to Israel, bearing presents of clothing, gold, and silver. He brought a lette asking for Naaman's healing from the king of Israel, written by the king of Aram. The king of Israel was upset because he thought he was being set up for defeat. However, Elisha, the prophet, stepped in and told Naaman to deep himself in the Jordan River seven times. Naaman was wroth because of Elisha's instruction, he wanted a better river but his servants encouraged him to obey the man of God. He obeyed and dipped himself seven times and his leprosy was healed, his skin was like the skin of a baby. What a mighty God we serve. He is the healer. Any embarrassing situation in your life today, is dealt with in the name of Jesus.

4. **Hezekiah's healing:**

In lsaiah 38: 1-8, King Hezekiah became gravely ill in his days. Prophet Isaiah son of Amoz was sent by God to tell King Hezekiah that he would not get better from his illness and that he should put his house in order because he was going to die. But Hezekiah turned his face away from the wall and prayed to the Lord fervently with painful tears, he reminded God of how he had been walking perfectly before the Lord with a true heart. The Lord heard his prayers and he was healed from his sickness and the Lord added fifteen more years to his years.

Healing is from the Lord, that is why He is called Jehovah Rapha, the Lord our healer. He healed yesterday, today and forever. The bible says whosoever shall call upon the name of the Lord shall be saved. Call upon God today, He is the great physician.

Healing in the New Testament:

God did not only heal in the Old Testament but also in the New Testament. Jesus performed healing miracles for everyone who came to Him and those He went to when He was on earth. He healed the blind, the lame, the deaf and those suffering from various infirmities. And Jesus went about all of Galilee, teaching in their synagogues, preaching the gospel of the kingdom, and curing all kinds of illnesses and diseases among the people, according to Matthew 4:23. Many who were sick came to Jesus. The book of Matthew 8:16 declares; *"When evening had come, they brought to Him many who were demon-possessed. And He cast out the spirits with a word, and healed all who were sick,"*

Examples of healing in the New Testament.

There are numerous outstanding instances of healing found in the New Testament. Here are a few noteworthy examples:

1. Peter's mother in-law was healed

In Mark Chapter 1:29-31, the bible says that Peter's mother in-law was in bed because she was sick of very high fever. Jesus was told about her sickness and He went to her bed-side and took her by the hand and assisted her to sit up and immediately she was healed. The bible recorded that in the evening after sunset, the sick and people who were demon possessed came to Jesus and Jesus healed many people who were sick with various diseases and many demons were casted out.

2. Jesus casted out an evil spirit

In Mark 1:21-28, there is an intriguing account of Jesus' authority and power that was demonstrated in a temple in Capernaum . On the Sabbath day Jesus and His disciples entered the synagogue and Jesus began to teach with divine authority and the people were astonished. Suddenly, a man who had an unclean spirit cried out, recognising Jesus as the "Holy One of God." The demon acknowledged Jesus' authority over it. Jesus rebuked the demon, commanding it to come out of the man. The demon convulsed the man but obeyed Jesus and left. The people were amazed at this display of authority over evil spirits. News about Jesus went around rapidly throughout the region.

This story revealed Jesus' power over spiritual forces and His unique authority as the Son of God. It sets the tone for His ministry of healing, deliverance, and teaching throughout the New Testament.

3. The woman with the issue of blood

n Matthew 9:20-22, the bible says there was a woman who had an issue of blood for 12 years. She went to many physicians and spent all that she had but instead of her matter getting better it grew worse. One day she heard about Jesus and she said in her heart that if only she could touch the hem of His garment, she would be made whole. She acted n faith and touched the hem of Jesus' garment and immediately her issue of blood seized. She was healed of her infirmity. When Jesus was touched by the woman Jesus realised

that virtue had gone out of Him and He asked who touched Him. The woman responded and Jesus said
her faith had made her whole. The woman was not just healed but made whole. What a mighty God we serve.

4. Centurion's servant healed

In Matthew 8:5-12 the bible says a centurion, a Roman officer, approached Jesus with a plea for his sick servant The centurion's faith stood out because he recognized Jesus authority and believed that a simple word from Him could heal his servant. His trust in Jesus' power surpassed wha Jesus had seen among the Israelites. Jesus was amazed by the centurion's faith. He praised it as exceptional, emphasis ing that even Gentiles (non-Israelites) would participate in the Kingdom of Heaven due to their faith. Jesus granted the centurion's request without physically going to the servan He commended the centurion's belief, and the servant wa healed instantly. This story revealed the importance of recognizing Jesus' authority. The centurion's faith serves as an inspiring example for all believers. The bible says all things are possible to him that believes.

It is evident from the bible that Jesus is the healer and He wants His children to demonstrate the supernatural power of healing.

In Matthew 28:18-19 the bible declares, *"[18] And Jesus came and spoke to them, saying, "All authority has been given to Me in heaven and on earth. [19] Go [a]therefore and make disciples of all the nations, baptising them in the name of the Father and of the Son and of the Holy Spirit,"*

Jesus' supernatural power is available to every believer that would believe in the word of God.

Do you believe that Jesus would heal you and use you for healing the sick? Believe the living word of God and you will see the Holy Spirit work the supernatural through you for the glory of the Lord.

Throughout His Word, God emphasises His desire for His children to live in divine health and a proper relationship with Him. Pay attention to these verses from the Bible as you walk by faith, expecting your miracle today. Romans 10:17 declares faith comes by hearing and hearing by the word of God and applying the word of God to oneself is the source of faith. An understanding of the Scriptures regarding healing is helpful in enabling us to believe God for the healing of our families, friends, and ourselves. These verses can fit on a piece of paper the size of a business card and be carried around.

Isaiah53:5 declares: *"But He was wounded for our transgressions, He was bruised for our iniquities; The chastisement for our peace was upon Him, And by His stripes we are healed."*

God is the Healer, and He always has been. "I am the Lord that healeth thee," His words declare. Living in divine health is what He desires for you. The God of miracles can make everything right in your life, no matter what you are going through right now. You can rely on Him to revitalise your youth and bring back your health, in Jesus mighty name.

CHAPTER 11

GOD IS ABLE TO EMPOWER.

God is omnipotent, He possesses unlimited authority and power. He is the Almighty God, the King of kings and the Lord of Lords.

The bible declares in Psalms 62:11;*"God has spoken once, Twice I have heard this:That power belongs to God."*

All power belongs to our God and He wants His children to partake of His power. In the book of Mathew Chapter 28:18-19, Jesus told His disciples that all authority has been given to Him in heaven and on earth and He instructed His disciples to go in His power. As Christians we are to operate in the supernatural and that is the reason the bible says, *"all things are ours"* (1 Corinthians 3:21).

When Jesus was leaving the earth to ascend to Heaven, He instructed His disciples in the book of Acts chapter 1 verse 4-5 to tarry in Jerusalem until they receive the promise of the father for the Holy Ghost. In obedience to Jesus's command the bible says that the disciples all met together and were constantly united in prayer.

On the day of Pentecost in Acts 2:1-4 the bible says the believers were in one accord in the upper room praying for the infilling of the Holy Ghost and suddenly there came a sound from Heaven like the roaring of a mighty wind and t filled the house where they were sitting. The bible says hat tongue of fire appeared and settled on each head of he disciples and everyone of them received the Holy Ghost with evidence of speaking in tongues as the Holy Spirit gave hem the ability.

After the disciples received the Holy Spirit, they began to

change their world. On the day of Pentecost, Peter, one of the disciples, preached to the crowd about Jesus and 3000 souls believed in the Lord Jesus and gave their lives to Jesus Christ (Acts 2:14- 41). Also, in Acts 3 Peter and John on their way to the temple at the hour of prayer, met a man at the beautiful gate that was crippled from birth who was a beggar. The lame man was expecting them to give him money but they told the lame man that silver or gold they had none but what they had was Jesus. They told the man to get up in the name of Jesus. Hallelujah, in the name of Jesus, he got up and he began to leap and praise the Lord. We serve a mighty God.

As the disciples began to walk with the Holy Spirit, they were filled again and again. In Acts 4:8 Peter was filled again with the Holy Ghost and in Acts 4:31; the bible says that after the disciples prayed the meeting place shook and they were all filled with the Holy Ghost and they preached the word of God with boldness.

It is important to look carefully at Acts:1:8 which says,

"But you shall receive power when the Holy Spirit has come upon you; and you shall be witnesses to Me in Jerusalem, and in all Judea and Samaria, and to the end of the earth."

After receiving the Holy Ghost with evidence of speaking in tongues, it is important to go higher so that one can be the best God has ordained one to be. The power of the Holy Ghost must follow the life of a Christian that is filled with the Holy Ghost with evidence of speaking in tongues. The word of God says we shall receive power after the Holy Ghost has come upon us. Every believer must be hungry for the power of the Holy Ghost. John 7 :37 says, "if any man thirst, let him come….." It is important to be hungry for the power of the Holy Ghost. The power of God takes a believer to the next level in God. Power of God is in levels.

Levels of Power of God

A. Power of God:

There is Power Of God, and God wants His children to operate in power. That is why Acts 1:8 says "ye shall receive power after the Holy Ghost

has come upon you…" Have you received the power of the Holy Ghost? To be an effective child of God we must receive the power of the Holy Ghost. Those who know their God shall be strong and do exploit. Never be satisfied with your level in God, ask for more. The more we seek Him the more we will find Him. Beloved of God, always be thirsty for more of God.

B. Great Power of God

As growing Christians, we must all seek the Lord for great

power from above. Great power will not accidentally come upon believers. It is our hunger for the Holy Spirit that will birth great power in our lives as believers. In Acts 1:14 the bible says that the disciples continued in prayers and supplication in one accord. The result of their prayers was evident in Acts 4:33 which says that the disciples witnessed about the resurrection of the Lord Jesus with great power and great grace was upon them.

C. Mighty Power of God

Another level of power in the word of God is mighty power. The bible says in Luke 9:43 that the people who witnessed how a demon possessed boy was healed and delivered by Jesus were all amazed by the mighty power of God. In Luke 9: 37-42 after coming down from the

mountain, Jesus and His disciples encountered a large crowd. Among them was a desperate father who pleaded with Jesus to heal his only son that was sick. The boy was tormented by an evil spirit that caused him to scream, convulse, and foam at the mouth. The disciples had tried to cast out the spirit but were unable to. Jesus commanded the father to bring his son forward and as the boy approached, the demon seized him, throwing him to the ground in a violent convulsion. Jesus rebuked the impure spirit, commanding it to leave the boy and the demon obeyed, and the boy was instantly healed.

Jesus then handed the restored child back to his overwhelmed father. The crowd witnessed this miraculous act, reinforcing Jesus' authority over evil forces and His compassion for those in need of healing. God wants His children to operate in mighty power from above.

D. Exceedingly Great Power

As God's children, the bible says that we have access to

exceedingly great power. In Ephesians:1:19 the bible says: *"and what is the exceeding greatness of His power toward us who believe, according to the working of His mighty power."*

This verse emphasises the extraordinary power available to believers.

E. Power without measure

Every believer must desire to operate with power without measure. This is the unlimited power available to every believer. John 3:34 says that Jesus had the power without measure. He performed miracles because of unlimited power upon His life. To do exploit for the Lord and be everything that God has called us to be, we must desire to operate in unlimited power.

How to receive power from the Lord:

The first step to receiving power of the Holy Ghost is to accept Jesus as Lord and saviour. Romans 10:9-10 says:

*“9 that if you confess with your mouth the Lord Jesus and
believe in your heart that God has raised Him from the
dead, you will be saved. 10 For with the heart one believes
unto righteousness, and with the mouth confession is
made unto salvation.”*

After accepting Jesus as Lord and Saviour, a Christian must continue to be born again. No looking back. Whoever shall endure to the end shall be saved and no man having put his hands to the plough and looking back the bible says such a person is not fit for the kingdom of God.(Luke 9:62).

As a born again Christian it is important to seek the Lord. Seeking the Lord is spending quality time in the word of God daily. John 1:1 says:

“In the beginning was the Word, and the Word was with God, and the Word was God.”

The word of God is God Himself and He is revealed to man through His word, the bible. It is vital to read, study meditate, memorise and obey the word of God. The more a believer will seek the Lord, the more God will revea

Himself to the person. If we seek Him, we will find Him. Spending time in God's word will increase the power of God on a believer.

Also, praying and fasting increase the power of God in believers' lives. Jesus told His disciples in Mark 9:29 that without praying and fasting, these things cannot be done. You want unlimited power of God, praying and fasting is crucial to accessing unlimited power of the Holy Ghost. The apostles operated in the unlimited power of the Holy Ghost because they gave themselves to seeking the Lord by praying and fasting. The bible says in Acts 1:14 that the apostles continued in seeking the Lord by continuing in praying.

In addition, to access the unlimited power of the Holy Ghost, a believer must have faith in God. The bible says have faith in God (Mark 11:22).

To operate under the supernatural, it is important to have

absolute faith in God. Hebrews 11:6 says,
"But without faith, it is impossible to please God, he that comes to God must believe that He is and He is a rewarder of those that diligently seek Him"

Seeking the Lord in faith, increases the anointing of God in a life.

Furthermore, daily praise and worship will increase the power of God in a Christian life. The bible says God inhabits the praises of His people(Psalms 22:3).

Also, fellowshipping with believers will increase the power of God in a believer's life. The word of God declares iron sharpens iron and deep things call unto deep things. (Proverbs:27:17). Regular fellowship with children of God increases the supernatural in believers life. To operate in the unlimited power of the Holy Ghost, a believer must never forsake the assembly of the saints.(Hebrews 10:25).

CHAPTER 12

CONCLUSION

Beloved of God, l believe the Holy Spirit has been touching your heart as you have been reading this ɔook and you are now convinced that the able God is able to lo great and mighty things in your life if only you can trust His words which are yea and amen. Rely on the living word ɔf God and you will see Him work wonders in your life.

God will never fail. He did not fail Abraham, Isaac and Jacob, He cannot start failing with you. Hold on to the Lord, He is well able to finish what He has started in your life.

hilippians: 1:6 says,
being confident of this very thing, that He who has beun a good work in you will complete it until the day of

Jesus Christ;"

Never, look at where you are right now, God has the power to do more in your life, He is well able to take you higher in the journey of life. Just let your focus be on Him and not challenges of life. He will never mismanage your life, He is the Almighty God that can do great and mighty things.

Dear child of God, there is more to your life, the able God will surely surprise you, in Jesus name. I see God taking you higher. You will surely

fulfil your destiny. The plans and purposes of God for you life shall come to manifestation in Jesus name.

GOD IS ABLE TO DO EXCEEDINGLY, ABUNDANTLY, ABOVE ALL THAT WE CAN ASK OR THINK, ACCORDING TO THE POWER THAT WORKS IN US HALLELUJAH.

I trust that this book has been a blessing to you.

We would love to hear your testimony on how it has impacted your life.

You can share with us via:

Phone: +44 (0) 20 7346 8673

Email: admin@bodyofchristchristiancentre.com.

IF YOU ARE NOT SAVED

YOU ARE NOTSAFE.

Jesus died for mankind because of the love of the father fo every man. The bible says in John 3:16 that God so loved th world that He gave His own beloved son, that whosoeve believes in Him shall not perish but will have eternal life. A life without Christ will be in crisis. Are you born again? If the answer is no or l am not sure, you need to accept Jesu as your Lord and Saviour. You must surrender to Jesus. Th greatest miracle is to be saved. Romans:10:9-10 says,

"[9] *that if you confess with your mouth the Lord Jesus an*
believe in your heart that God has raised Him from th
dead, you will be saved. [10] *For with the heart one believe*
unto righteousness, and with the mouth confession is mad
unto salvation."

Please say this simple prayer with all your heart.

Lord Jesus, l come before you today. I am a sinner, l cannot save myself. Jesus forgive me my sins and wash me with your precious blood. I surrender myself to you.

I accept you as my Lord and Saviour.

Thank you Jesus for saving me. Now l am born again, Hallelujah.

www.ingramcontent.com/pod-product-compliance
Lightning Source LLC
LaVergne TN
LVHW010109170826
845678LV00012B/2310

* 9 7 8 1 9 0 8 2 2 8 1 0 9 *